❖ GREAT LITTLE COOK BOOKS ❖

Indonesian
COOKING

Kusuma Widjaya/Roland Marske

Brilliant colours and exotic aromas,

tropical rain forests, luxuriant gardens and
a colourful population mix: that's Indonesia.
Indonesian cuisine reflects the wonderfully
varied landscape and the living culture of these
far-away islands. Let yourself be taken on a culinary
journey through the Indonesian archipelago –
and you will get to know Asia's most
exciting cookery!

Colour photographs by
Odette Teubner and Dorothee Gödert.

AURA

A magical landscape and a tropical paradise: water, islands and luxuriant vegetation.

both Indonesia consists of thousands of tropical islands, including the well-known, larger ones of Java, Bali, Sumatra and Borneo. However, of the 17,000 islands, only 4,000 are inhabited – by more than 180 million people. They form a lively population mix, with many different traditions and languages, influenced from very early on by foreign cultures. First came Chinese traders, who had the strongest cultural influence on Indonesia. They were then followed by Indian seafarers, who brought Buddhism and Hinduism. Later, Arab merchants and scholars imported Islam.

The political history of Indonesia has also been one of changes. The islands belonged first to the Portuguese, then to the Dutch, who remained there for 250 years. Although the Indonesians had to engage in a bloody battle for their independence, they always remained open to foreign influences. However, they have never simply adopted new ideas, but always adapted them to their individual needs.

Indonesian cooking
The countless foreign influences that affected Indonesia during its history helped to create the most varied traditions. This gave rise to a cuisine that is among the most versatile in the world.

Paradoxically, Indonesian cooking is full of contrasts, yet also full of harmony. Mild curries that are fragrant with exotic sauces and lemon grass and rich with creamy coconut milk are accompanied by sambals – fiery dishes prepared with plenty of hot chillies. Sweet, sour and salty are constantly combined. Harmony and balance of flavours and textures are the aims. So, for example, soft rice dishes and salads are served with small, crispy fried canapés.

Chinese influences

The Chinese have traded with the Indonesians for thousands of years and many of them have also settled in Indonesia. Indonesian cuisine has taken more from them than any other foreign country. For a start, the Chinese brought wholly new ingredients with them, such as spinach, aubergines, cucumbers and tofu. The Indonesians are also indebted to them for their most important cooking utensil, a rounded metal pan, called a wok in China and a *kuali* or *wajan* in Indonesia. They took over the art of cooking in it at the same time. In wok cookery, it is important to keep the particular flavour of each individual ingredient as unspoilt as possible. So, following Chinese cuisine, the dishes are cooked for only a short time. However, the generous use of chillies makes it clear that the dish is unmistakably Indonesian.

Indian influences

Indian influences show not only in the large-scale use of spices and aromatic flavourings, but also in the preparation of curries. For these, meat or vegetables are cooked slowly in a spicy sauce. The combination of spices is almost identical in both countries, but, while the Indians like to use yogurt for their sauces, Indonesian curries are characteristically flavoured with the distinctive note of coconut milk. This is made from the flesh of young coconuts, which is grated and squeezed to extract the milk used for cooking.

As many Hindus and all Buddhists are vegetarian, Indonesian cuisine traditionally incorporates a wide range of delicious vegetable dishes. As meat is usually expensive and, in some parts of the country, it is very difficult to rear animals, this aspect of Indonesian cooking has been perfected over many centuries.

Islamic influences

Islamic influence can be seen not only in Indonesian social life, but also in its culinary tradition. About ninety percent of Indonesians are Muslims, so pork, which is forbidden in the Koran, is absent from most Indonesian menus, except on Bali and, of course, among the Chinese and Christian communities. (In fact, on Bali, pork is the meat most frequently prepared for festivals and special occasions.) The Islamic fasting month of Ramadan, during which nothing is eaten or drunk between sunrise and sunset, is strictly observed by many Indonesians.

Dutch influences

The Dutch enriched Indonesian cooking mainly by introducing new kinds of vegetables. Many of these vegetables still keep their Dutch names – *kol*

Chinese heritage: the wok, a semi-circular, metal cooking pan. It is the most important utensil in Indonesian cooking. All the ingredients can be cooked quickly and so retain their nutrients and their own particular flavour and texture.

(cabbage), *buncis* (beans), *wortel* (carrots) and *tomat* (tomato), for example. Otherwise Dutch influence on Indonesian cuisine was fairly small. On the other hand, the Dutch were greatly inspired by Indonesian cooking and brought one of it greatest delicacies, the *rijsttafel* or rice-table to Europe. Many ex-patriate Indonesians live in Holland and the consequent flourishing restaurant trade has now spread to many other parts of Northern Europe.

Regional specialities

The cuisine of a country with a mixed population, which is also made up of many islands, naturally has many regional specialities. Whereas for people living on the coast, the sea is the chief provider of fresh food, the people who live inland usually dry fish and seafood. Although many people who live inland enrich their diet by breeding fish in the flooded rice fields, their main foodstuffs are generally limited to what they can grow themselves, particularly rice and some vegetables around the edges of the paddy fields. Most of the islands produce two or even three crops of rice each year. Madura is the exception, its low rainfall allowing only one and, occasionally, two crops.

In the impenetrable rain forest areas, the food supply is different again. Here, gathering fruits, nuts and roots plays an important part. Meat is too

Fresh fish is abundant in the coastal regions. It is rare inland, so many peasants breed fish in their flooded rice fields.

expensive for most of the population. Although they do enjoy eating it, they eat very much less meat than Europeans and Americans.

The most famous cuisine in Indonesia is the Padang cookery of Western Sumatra. Throughout Indonesia there are many restaurants offering Padang cuisine, all of them recognizable from the numerous mouth-burningly hot dishes displayed in their windows. Diners each receive a small bowl of each of these dishes or help themselves to whichever ones appeal. Dining out on warm, tropical evenings is a universal pleasure.

Javanese cooking is also widespread throughout Indonesia and many restaurants on the other islands are often run by Javanese. (Java is the principal island on which the capital, Jakarta, is situated.) The dishes are quite mild and slightly sweet because they are always prepared with palm sugar. In fact, in Indonesia, palm sugar is called *gula jawa* – literally, sweet Java. The Javanese love of sweet things is also shown in their wonderfully exotic sweets and desserts, which are created from the most varied combinations of rice, coconut and palm sugar.

The most versatile and colourful Indonesian cuisine is inarguably Balinese. Every conceivable kind of fruit and vegetable grows in tropical abundance on this most beautiful island's fertile volcanic soil. The sea provides huge quantities of fish and because the Balinese are not Muslims, but Hindus, they are very fond of pork. Celebrations and festivals seem to take place on Bali with astonishing frequency and food, of course, plays a special role on these occasions. Outdoor cooking on a barbecue is popular in this tropical paradise and fish is often sold already threaded on bamboo skewers.

The cuisine of Sulawesi also deserves mention. It is very varied because of the many different peoples who live on this island and is, perhaps, the most exotic in the whole of Indonesia: goldfish, dogs, bats and snakes enrich its menu – although no recipes calling for quite such unusual ingredients are included in this book.

But throughout Indonesia, as everywhere else in South Asia, rice is the staple food. The Indonesians are familiar with countless varieties of rice and even more ways of preparing it and it is served with virtually every meal. Only on Timor is maize preferred to rice. In the Molukks and Irian Jaya, manioc, the starch-rich root bulb of a spurge plant, and the tapioca made from it are the traditional staple food.

Sticky or long grain, spiced or plain, rice is the staple food of Indonesians. It is cultivated on almost all the inhabited islands in extensive fields or on terraces – exhaustingly hard work, which is mainly undertaken by women.

The Rijsttafel

The whole range of Indonesian cookery is displayed in the famous rijsttafel – the rice table. The name comes from the Dutch colonial period, when lavish banquets were held in Indonesia. Such banquets, called Selamatan by the Indonesians, are still held in extravagant splendour at religious festivals and at the end of the harvest or rainy season.

People sit companionably at long tables with enormous bowls of rice on them. Between 30 and 40 different meat, fish and vegetable dishes are served. People at the table each help themselves to rice in a wide-brimmed bowl, spoon over some soup or broth to moisten it and then select a little of whichever other dishes they would like to taste, one after the other.

Refreshment on the street: juicy fruit and brightly coloured soft drinks are favourite thirst-quenchers throughout Indonesia.

Drinks

At Indonesian meals, the usual drink is water or sweetened tea, although tourists will often be offered soft drinks or beer. Alcoholic drinks are served only on special occasions. On the islands where most of the inhabitants are Muslims, alcohol is forbidden, but often this applies only to Western spirits. Most Indonesians are reluctant to give up their own home-made drinks. The best known of these are the various rather mild kinds of *tuak* (palm wine) and *brem* (rice wine), whose high alcohol content cannot be tasted and is, therefore, felt all the more rapidly.

Arak (rice brandy) is distilled from *brem*; this is best drunk in coffee. Beer, produced under licence by various European breweries, is mainly available in tourist centres. Dutch influence is again apparent both in the taste of the light, malty lager and in the squat shape of the bottles. Asia's first brewery, set up in the Philippines, also produces beer in Indonesia. As few bars have refrigeration, beer is either served warm or with ice cut from a block.

The choice of non-alcoholic drinks, on the other hand, is impressive. As well as well-known international brands, there are fragrant, imaginative drinks in the most remarkable colours, often made with coconut milk, fruit and indefinable slippery ingredients. Instead of these local drinks, tourists often prefer fresh milk from young coconuts and raw sugar juice.

Meals at home

Ordinary home-cooked meals, on the other hand, are usually very simple, but they always consist of some kind of rice table, as rice is at the centre of every meal. A meal would be considered incomplete without it. It is served with two or three meat, fish or vegetable dishes and a selection of spicy sauces, intended to make the rice tasty. The dishes are always served at the same time. Apart from dessert, Indonesian meals are not divided into separate courses in the way that Western meals are. Everyone helps themselves first to rice and then surrounds it with small portions of the other dishes.

Simple desserts – usually rice- or fruit-based – and fresh fruit are always served at the end of a meal.

If guests are invited, a larger selection of dishes is served as a mark of hospitality. People eat off plates, often large, shallow soup plates, or banana leaves and not from small bowls as in China. The food is carried to the mouth either with a spoon and fork or simply with the fingers of the right hand (not too difficult if the rice is sticky). As in most of South-east Asia, any dish may be served at any time of day. Breakfast, lunch and dinner differ only in quantity, dinner being the most important meal, when the whole family gathers together.

Typical ingredients

You can buy virtually everything you need for Indonesian cooking in Chinese and Asian supermarkets, which can now be found in nearly every large city. Some other shops and large supermarkets also stock quite a sizeable range of Asian ingredients and spices.

If you want to cook Indonesian food frequently, you should collect a small stock of the ingredients which appear in most of the recipes. It is not always easy to understand what is written on the packets of many products in Asian shops, but you can always ask the shopkeeper's advice and use the following list as an aid to your shopping.

Agar-agar
A thickener made from seaweed or algae, it can be used like gelatine. It is available in transparent sticks about 30 cm/12 inches long or as powder in various colours. The sticks must be chopped up and softened in water before use. You can also buy agar-agar from health food shops.

Banana leaves
(Daun pisang)
The giant leaves of the banana plant are extremely practical. They are used to wrap up fillings before grilling, boiling or steaming, making a neat parcel and adding additional flavour. Plunge them briefly into boiling water before using to make them more pliable. Secure the parcels with a cocktail stick or a fine skewer. The leaves themselves are not eaten. They are available frozen or dried.

Coconut milk
(Santen)
This is not the clear liquid found inside the coconut. Coconut milk is made from the grated flesh of young coconuts. Its taste and aroma are like nothing else and so it should not be replaced by any other ingredient. You can make coconut milk yourself. Pour 475 ml/16 fl oz boiling water on to 500 g/1 1/4 lb grated coconut and set aside to soak until the water has cooled completely. Process the mixture in a food processor and pass it through a fine strainer. You can buy instant coconut milk in powdered form, blocks of creamed coconut and cans of coconut milk that is ready to use. Canned coconut milk is very practical, but must be used quickly once the can has been opened. However, you can freeze left-over canned coconut milk.

Galangal
(Laos)
A spicy root similar to ginger to which it is related, this is also known as Thai ginger. It is milder, but sourer than ginger. Prepare it in the same way as

Fresh from the market – fruits, vegetables and spices.

9

fresh root ginger, making sure that it is thoroughly peeled as the skin has an unpleasant taste. You can also buy it ground as laos powder, but this does not have such a good flavour as fresh. Use 5 ml/1 teaspoon powder as a substitute for every 2.5 cm/1 inch fresh root.

Ginger
(Jahe)
An indispensable spice in Indonesian cuisine, the fresh root can be bought all the year round and it will keep for 3–4 weeks in the refrigerator. Ginger is often stir-fried with onions and garlic, so ground ginger is no substitute, as it turns bitter when it is fried.

Lemon grass
(Sereh)
This reed-like thick grass contains strong volatile oils smelling of lemon. Unless otherwise indicated, only the soft thick lower part of the stalk is used for cooking. If the lemon grass is not completely fresh, the dry outer leaves must be removed.

Macadamia nuts
(Kemiri nuts)
These cream-coloured nuts are grated to thicken and add aroma to curries and soups.

They have a very hard shell, making them difficult to crack, so it is best to buy them already shelled. Otherwise, you can use almonds or Brazil nuts.

Palm sugar
(Gula jawa, Gula mekka)
This is made from the juice of the coconut palm or the sugar palm and should not be replaced by ordinary sugar because it has an inimitable aroma. For most recipes, unless otherwise instructed, you need the easy-to-use crystalline palm sugar. You can also buy palm sugar as a paste.

Rice flour
Fine flour made from white rice is used for sweet dishes. You can also buy it in health food shops.

Sambal ulek
(Sambal ulek)
A fiery hot classical Indonesian spice made from pounded chillies, oil and salt, it is used in nearly every dish. As well as sambal ulek, you can buy all kinds of other Indonesian spicy pastes under the general name of sambals. A small selection of them for individual seasoning of the dishes goes well with every Indonesian meal.

Shrimp paste
(Terasi)
Every Asian country has its own fish paste. Indonesian terasi is made from pounded dried shrimp and can be obtained raw or roasted. It is strong tasting, so use in only small quantities. In the recipes in this book, only the milder roasted form of terasi is used.

Delicious, unique and typically Indonesian – coconut milk and flesh.

Chillies are an indispensable ingredient in Indonesian cooking.

Soy sauce
(Kecap asin)
A spicy, very salty sauce made from fermented soya beans, wheat, salt and water, it can be used for seasoning.

Sticky rice
(Ketan)
This very starchy short grain variety of rice becomes sticky when cooked and so is good for eating with the fingers, which is still sometimes the custom in Indonesia. Sticky rice is very filling.

Sweet soy sauce
(Kecap manis)
Thick, sweet Indonesian variety of soy sauce.

Tamarind
(Asam)
These brown bean-like pulses grow on trees. Their sweet-sour juice is used for acidulation in the way Western cooks use vinegar or lemon juice. You can buy tamarind in concentrated blocks and store them in the refrigerator.

Tempeh
(Tempe)
This traditional Indonesian product made out of fermented soya beans is often called soya bread. Tempeh has a slightly fermented taste, which disappears when it is fried. It consists of 50 percent high-quality protein. You can buy it in Chinese shops.

Tofu
(Tahu)
This product made from soya milk is also known as bean curd. It is prized by vegetarians as a meat substitute because of its high protein content and versatility in absorbing other flavours. You can buy tofu fresh, smoked or marinated.

Turmeric
(Kunyit)
A bright yellow spice made from a root similar to ginger, it is usually sold ground. Because of its colour it is often used instead of the much more expensive saffron. As it has a bitter taste, use turmeric only in very small quantities. It is an important ingredient in curry.

White rice

Nasi putih

Easy

Serves 4
*300 g/11 oz fragrant rice or long
    grain rice*
600 ml/1 pint water
salt

Approximately per portion:
1,000 kJ/240 kcal
5 g protein, 0 g fat
59 g carbohydrate

● Approximate preparation
   time: 30 minutes

---

1. Rinse the rice in a strainer and briefly drain it. Put the rice, water and a pinch of salt into a saucepan with a tight-fitting lid. Bring to the boil, uncovered, over a high heat.

2. As soon as the water boils, reduce the heat. Cover and cook over a low heat for 15–20 minutes.

3. When the rice has absorbed all the water, remove the saucepan from the heat and set aside, covered, for a further 10 minutes before serving.

Tip

If you want to cook more or less rice, follow the rule of thumb: 1 cup of rice to 2 cups of water.

Yellow rice

Nasi kuning

For guests

Serves 4
300 g/11 oz long grain rice
2.5 ml/¹/2 teaspoon ground turmeric
600 ml/1 pint water
2 stalks of lemon grass
1 cinnamon stick
salt

Approximately per portion:
1,000 kJ/240 kcal
5 g protein, 0 g fat
59 g carbohydrate

● Approximate preparation
   time: 30 minutes

---

1. Rinse the rice in a strainer under cold running water until the water runs clear. Drain well. Put the rice, turmeric and water into a saucepan with a tight-fitting lid. Cut the lemon grass into large pieces and add it to the pan, together with the cinnamon. Bring to the boil, uncovered, over a high heat.

2. As soon as the water boils, reduce the heat. Cover and cook over a low heat for 15–20 minutes.

3. When the rice has absorbed all the water, remove the pan from the heat. Set aside, covered, for a further 10 minutes. Remove and discard the lemon grass and cinnamon before serving.

Coconut rice

Nasi uduk

Exquisite

Serves 4
300 g/11 oz long grain rice
400 ml/14 fl oz coconut milk
200 ml/7 fl oz water
salt

Approximately per portion:
1,000 kJ/240 kcal
6 g protein, 0 g fat
60 g carbohydrate

● Approximate preparation
   time: 30 minutes

---

1. Rinse the rice in a strainer and briefly drain it. Put the rice, coconut milk, water and a pinch of salt into a saucepan with a tight-fitting lid. Bring to the boil, uncovered, over a high heat.

2. As soon as the liquid boils, reduce the heat. Cover and cook the rice over a low heat for 15–20 minutes.

3. When the rice has completely absorbed the liquid, remove the pan from the heat. Set aside, covered, to stand for a further 10 minutes before serving.

Above: White rice
Centre: Yellow rice
Below: Coconut rice

Sticky rice

Ketan

As the name indicates, this kind of rice sticks together when it is cooked. This is particularly practical if the meal is eaten with the fingers, as is still sometimes the custom in Indonesia. It is easier to pick up mouthfuls of it than rice that remains grainy when cooked. Sticky rice is usually eaten lukewarm with hot meat dishes.

Quick

Serves 4
250 g/9 oz sticky rice
500 ml/18 fl oz water
salt

Approximately per portion:
840 kJ/200 kcal
4 g protein, 0 g fat
49 g carbohydrate

● Approximate preparation
 time: 20 minutes

---

1. Rinse the sticky rice in a strainer and briefly drain it. Put it into a saucepan with a tight-fitting lid. Pour in the water, add a pinch of salt and bring to the boil, uncovered, over a high heat.

2. As soon as the water boils, reduce the heat. Cover and cook over a low heat for about 10 minutes.

3. When the rice has completely absorbed the water, remove the saucepan from the heat. Set aside, covered, to stand for a further 10 minutes before serving.

Rice in banana leaf rolls

Lontong

If you cannot obtain a banana leaf, you can use aluminium foil instead in this recipe.

Can be prepared in advance

Makes 20 rice rolls
1 banana leaf
300 g/11 oz sticky rice
salt

Approximately per roll:
200 kJ/48 kcal
1 g protein, 0 g fat
12 g carbohydrate

● Approximate preparation
 time: 1 hour

---

1. Thaw the banana leaf, if frozen, blanch briefly in boiling water, if wished and cut it into twenty 15 × 15 cm/6 × 6 inch squares.

2. Roll up each square into a cylinder and fasten one end with half a cocktail stick (if you are substituting aluminium foil, use a double thickness).

3. Rinse the rice in a strainer and briefly drain it. Fill each banana leaf roll one third full. Do not add more rice than this because it needs space to expand. Fasten the other end of each roll with half a cocktail stick.

4. Arrange the stuffed banana leaf rolls closely side by side in a saucepan. Pour in enough water to cover the rolls by 1 cm/½ inch. Add salt, cover and cook for about 45 minutes over a medium heat, until the rice has absorbed the liquid completely and the banana rolls are full to overflowing.

5. Remove the rice rolls from the pan and set aside to cool slightly. This makes the rice stick together in a compact block. You can slice the rice rolls, using a sharp knife, with or without the leaf still wrapped around them. Serve them with meat dishes and soups. The banana leaves are not eaten.

Tip

If you are in a hurry, prepare the rice rolls the day before and steam them for 20 minutes, until warmed through.

Above: Sticky rice
Below: Rice in banana leaf rolls

Skewered beef with peanut sauce

Sate daging

Rather time-consuming

Serves 4
750 g/1 lb 10 oz lean steak
rice, to serve
For the marinade:
45 ml/3 tablespoons sweet soy
    sauce (kecap manis)
45 ml/3 tablespoons soy sauce
5 ml/1 teaspoon sambal ulek
For the peanut sauce:
200 g/7 oz roasted, salted peanuts
2.5 cm/1 inch piece of fresh
    root ginger
45 ml/3 tablespoons vegetable oil
400 ml/14 fl oz coconut milk
juice of 1/2 lemon
45 ml/3 tablespoons sweet soy
    sauce (kecap manis)
15 ml/1 tablespoon soy sauce
15 ml/1 tablespoon palm sugar
2.5 ml/1/2 teaspoon sambal ulek

Approximately per portion:
2,500 kJ/600 kcal
51 g protein, 39 g fat
11 g carbohydrate

● Approximate preparation
   time: 2 hours of which
   1 hour is marinating time

1. Cut the steak into 1 cm/1/2 inch cubes. Thread 4 cubes of meat, spaced slightly apart, on to each of 40 wooden skewers.

2. Press the skewers flat with your hand and arrange side by side in a shallow dish.

3. To make the marinade, mix together the sweet soy sauce, soy sauce and sambal ulek. Spoon the mixture over the skewered steak, cover and marinate in the refrigerator, turning occasionally, for at least 1 hour.

4. To make the peanut sauce, pound the peanuts in a mortar with a pestle or process them in a food processor until finely ground. Finely grate the ginger.

5. Heat the vegetable oil in a saucepan. Add the ground peanuts and the ginger and stir-fry over a medium heat for about 2 minutes.

Variation:
You can use other kinds of meat, such as lamb (sate kambing), pork (sate babi) or chicken (sate ayam). Prawns (sate udang) or tofu (sate tahu) are also absolutely delicious cooked this way.

6. Add the coconut milk, lemon juice, sweet soy sauce, soy sauce, palm sugar and sambal ulek and simmer over a low heat, stirring occasionally, for about 10 minutes, until the sauce acquires the consistency of mayonnaise.

Tip

These steak skewers are ideal for cooking over a barbecue, when they can be served with a cold rice salad for a substantial and tasty meal.

7. Remove the skewers from the marinade and drain. Roast them in a preheated oven at 240°C/475°F/ Gas 9 for about 5–7 minutes, until the meat is browned. Alternatively, fry them in a frying pan over a medium heat until they are browned all over.

8. Pour the lukewarm peanut sauce over the steak skewers and serve with rice.

Vegetable salad with peanut sauce

Gado gado

Gado gado is a delicious light summer salad or, if it is served with rice, it is a complete vegetarian meal. Served warm, it is the ideal dish for an informal lunchtime party, when a double quantity can be prepared and presented on a large serving platter lined with a banana leaf.

Rather time-consuming •
For guests

Serves 4
150 g/5 oz green beans
1 carrot
250 g/9 oz fresh beansprouts
1 bunch of watercress or 115 g/
    4 oz lamb's lettuce
75 g/3 oz white cabbage leaves
1 small leek
1 litre/1 3/4 pints water
1/2 small cucumber
1 yellow or orange pepper
4 hard-boiled eggs, shelled
    and quartered
salt
For the peanut sauce:
200 g/7 oz roasted peanuts
2.5 cm/1 inch piece of fresh
    root ginger
45 ml/3 tablespoons groundnut or
    sunflower oil
400 ml/14 fl oz coconut milk
juice of 1/2 lemon
45 ml/3 tablespoons sweet soy
    sauce (kecap manis)
15 ml/1 tablespoon soy sauce
15 ml/1 tablespoon palm sugar
2.5 ml/1/2 teaspoon sambal
    ulek

Approximately per portion:
2,200 kJ/520 kcal
26 g protein, 38 g fat
16 g carbohydrate

● Approximate preparation
    time: 1 hour

1. Trim the beans and cut them into 5 cm/2 inch long pieces. Thinly slice the carrot.

2. Rinse and drain the beansprouts, watercress and the cabbage leaves. Cut the cabbage leaves into bite-size pieces. Thinly slice the leek. Bring the water to the boil in a large saucepan and add a generous pinch of salt.

3. Blanch the cabbage leaves, then the sliced leek and, finally, the beansprouts for about 3 minutes each in the boiling water, then thoroughly drain them. Add the beans and carrots to the pan and cook for about 5 minutes, until they are tender, but still firm to the bite. Drain well.

4. Peel and thinly slice the cucumber. Core and seed the pepper and cut the flesh into thin strips.

5. To make the peanut sauce, put the peanuts in a food processor and process until finely ground. Finely grate the root ginger.

6. Heat the oil in a saucepan. Add the ground peanuts and ginger and stir-fry over a medium heat for about 2 minutes.

7. Stir in the coconut milk, lemon juice, sweet soy sauce, soy sauce, palm sugar and sambal ulek. Reduce the heat and simmer the sauce over a low heat, stirring occasionally, for about 10 minutes, until it acquires the consistency of mayonnaise.

8. Divide the vegetables and eggs between four serving plates and pour the peanut sauce over them. Serve warm.

Variation:
You can alter the selection of vegetables to suit your taste. For example, potatoes, cauliflower, broccoli, canned sweetcorn and fresh spinach all taste delicious. Instead of eggs, you can use fried tofu slices or tofu balls.

An unusual combination, which you absolutely must try – crispy fresh vegetables and a creamy peanut sauce.

Fried noodles

Mie goreng

Easy

Serves 4
400 g/14 oz egg noodles
250 g/9 oz boneless pork loin
250g/9 oz broccoli
4 Chinese cabbage leaves
1 carrot
1 medium onion
2 cloves garlic
2.5 cm/1 inch piece of fresh
*   root ginger*
1.5 ml/1/4 teaspoon dried shrimp
*   paste (terasi)*
45 ml/3 tablespoons vegetable oil
1.5–2.5 ml/1/4–1/2 teaspoon sambal
*   ulek*
30 ml/2 tablespoons soy sauce
10 ml/2 teaspoons palm sugar
sweet soy sauce (kecap manis)

Approximately per portion:
2,300 kJ/550 kcal
30 g protein, 15 g fat
76 g carbohydrate

● Approximate preparation
  time: 35–45 minutes

1. Cook the noodles according to the instructions on the packet. Drain and rinse in cold water.

2. Bring a saucepan of well-salted water to the boil. Cut the pork into thin strips. Divide the broccoli into florets and briefly blanch them in the boiling water. Rinse in cold water and drain.

3. Cut the Chinese cabbage leaves into thin strips. Cut the carrot into matchsticks. Dice the onion and crush the garlic. Finely grate the ginger. Mash the shrimp paste.

4. Heat the vegetable oil in a preheated wok. Add the pork, onion, garlic, ginger, shrimp paste and sambal ulek. Stir-fry over a high heat for 3 minutes.

5. Add the broccoli and the Chinese cabbage leaves and stir-fry for 1 further minute. Mix in the noodles, soy sauce and palm sugar and stir-fry for a further 3 minutes. Season with the sweet soy sauce and serve immediately.

Fried rice

Nasi goreng

Make sure the rice is completely dry before you add it to the wok.

Most famous Indonesian dish

Serves 4
250 g/9 oz skinless, boneless
*   chicken breasts*
1/2 bunch spring onions
1 small red pepper
2 cloves garlic
75 ml/5 tablespoons vegetable oil
2 eggs
1.5–5 ml/1/4 –1 teaspoon sambal
*   ulek*
200 g/7 oz peeled cooked prawns
675 g/1 1/2 lb boiled rice, cooled
45 ml/3 tablespoons soy sauce
30 ml/2 tablespoons tomato
*   ketchup*
sweet soy sauce (kecap manis)
For the garnish:
1/4 small cucumber
60 ml/4 tablespoons deep-
*   fried onions*

Approximately per portion:
2,100 kJ/500 kcal
33 g protein, 16 g fat
64 g carbohydrate

● Approximate preparation
  time: 40 minutes

1. Cut the chicken into thin strips. Cut the green parts of the spring onions into 4 cm/1 1/2 inch long pieces and cut the white parts into thin rings. Core and seed the pepper and cut the flesh into strips. Crush the garlic.

2. Heat the vegetable oil in a preheated wok. Beat the eggs, add them to the wok and fry, stirring occasionally, until set into an omelette. Slide the omelette out of the wok on to a plate, set aside to cool and then cut it into strips.

3. Add the chicken strips, spring onions, pepper, garlic and sambal ulek to the wok and stir-fry over a high heat for about 2 minutes. Add the prawns and stir-fry for 1 further minute. Mix in the rice and soy sauce and stir-fry for about 3 minutes.

4. Remove the wok from the heat, mix in the tomato ketchup and the omelette strips, season with the sweet soy sauce and transfer to a serving dish. Peel and thinly slice the cucumber. Garnish the rice with the cucumber and deep-fried onions and serve immediately.

Above: Fried rice
Below: Fried noodles

Cucumber salad

Ketimum asam manis

This refreshing salad is an excellent accompaniment to fiery hot dishes and nasi goreng.

Quick • Economical

Serves 4
1 medium cucumber
30 ml/2 tablespoon palm sugar
30 ml/2 tablespoons vinegar
15 ml/1 tablespoon chopped
*   peppermint*
salt

Approximately per portion:
150 kJ/36 kcal
1 g protein, 0 g fat
8 g carbohydrate

● Approximate preparation
   time: 10 minutes

---

1. Peel the cucumber, cut it in half lengthways and scoop out the seeds with a teaspoon. Cut the cucumber halves into thin slices and put them into a bowl.

2. Thoroughly mix together the palm sugar, vinegar and peppermint and season with salt to taste in a small bowl.

3. Pour the dressing over the cucumber slices and toss well to mix. Serve at room temperature.

Chicken soup with coconut milk

Sato ayam santen

In Western restaurants, this spicy soup is usually served as a starter. If you serve it with rice, as is the usual way in Indonesia, it makes a complete meal.

Can be prepared in advance

Serves 4
2.5 cm/1 inch piece of fresh
*   root ginger*
3 stalks of lemon grass
800 g/1³/4 lb chicken
5 kaffir lime leaves
10 macadamia nuts
50 g/2 oz cellophane noodles
115 g/4 oz fresh beansprouts
1.5 ml/¹/4 teaspoon sambal ulek
2.5 ml/¹/2 teaspoon ground turmeric
45 ml/3 tablespoons lemon juice
400 ml/14 fl oz coconut milk
salt
60 ml/4 tablespoons deep-fried
*   onions, to garnish*

Approximately per portion:
1,900 kJ/450 kcal
40 g protein, 25 g fat
13 g carbohydrate

● Approximate preparation
   time: 1¹/4 hours

---

1. Finely grate the ginger. Cut the thick lower ends of the lemon grass into wafer-thin slices. Put the chicken in a large saucepan and cover with water. Add the ginger, lemon grass,

kaffir lime leaves and salt to taste. Cover, bring to the boil and cook over a high heat for about 30 minutes.

2. Meanwhile, bring another saucepan of water to the boil. Finely grate the macadamia nuts. Cut the noodles in 5 cm/2 inch long strips with kitchen scissors. Briefly blanch the beansprouts in the boiling water and drain.

3. Remove the chicken from the pan and set aside to cool, reserving the cooking liquid. Remove and discard the skin from the chicken, cut the meat from the bones and chop it finely.

4. Put the chicken, nuts, noodles and beansprouts into the reserved cooking liquid and bring to the boil. Season with the sambal ulek, turmeric and lemon juice and add the coconut milk. Cover and simmer over a low heat for about 10 minutes.

5. Remove and discard the kaffir lime leaves. Divide the soup between four individual soup bowls. Sprinkle with the deep-fried onions and serve immediately.

Above: Chicken soup with coconut milk
Below: Cucumber salad

Fried hot prawns

Sambal goreng udang

Rather expensive • Quick

Serves 4
1 onion
2 cloves garlic
about 2 cm/3/4 inch fresh galangal
*   or fresh root ginger*
2 fresh red chillies, each about
*   10 cm/4 inches long*
30 ml/2 tablespoons vegetable oil
500 g/1 1/4 lb peeled, cooked prawns
150 ml/1/4 pint coconut milk
5 ml/1 teaspoon ground coriander
salt

Approximately per portion:
730 kJ/170 kcal
22 g protein, 8 g fat
3 g carbohydrate

● Approximate preparation
   time: 25 minutes

---

1. Dice the onion. Finely grate the galangal or ginger. Seed the chillies and cut them into thin strips.

2. Heat the vegetable oil in a preheated wok or large frying pan. Add the onion, garlic, galangal or ginger and chillies and stir-fry over a medium heat until the onion is light golden brown.

3. Add the prawns. Reduce the heat and add the coconut milk, coriander and salt to taste and simmer over a low heat for about 5 minutes. Transfer to a warm serving dish and serve immediately.

Bananas in batter

Pisang goreng

Quick

Serves 4
12 baby bananas or 4 firm
*   large bananas*
For the batter:
25 g/1 oz butter
105 ml/7 tablespoons coconut
*   milk*
75 g/3 oz rice flour
10 ml/2 teaspoons sugar
45 ml/3 tablespoons grated
*   coconut*
salt
For frying:
75 ml/5 tablespoons vegetable
*   oil*

Approximately per portion:
1,900 kJ/450 kcal
3 g protein, 26 g fat
54 g carbohydrate

● Approximate preparation
   time: 20 minutes

---

1. Peel the bananas. Cut large bananas into two or three equal-size pieces. Melt the butter in a small saucepan over a low heat.

2. Put the coconut milk, rice flour, sugar, grated coconut, melted butter and a pinch of salt into a bowl. Beat thoroughly with a hand-held electric mixer to make a smooth batter.

3. Heat the vegetable oil in a large saucepan or a deep-fat fryer. Coat

the bananas in the batter and deep-fry them, a few at a time, for about 4 minutes, until golden. Remove the bananas, drain well on kitchen paper and serve.

Variation
Instead of bananas you can use fresh or canned pineapple chunks or slices.

Above: Fried hot prawns
Below: Bananas in batter

Sweet-and-sour pork

Babi asam manis

This is not just a Chinese favourite. Virtually every country in South-east Asia has its own version of this ever-popular dish.

Quick

Serves 4
2 tomatoes
15 ml/1 tablespoon tamarind pulp
150 ml/1/4 pint warm water
600 g/1 lb 5 oz lean, boneless pork, such as fillet
1 onion
2 cloves garlic
2.5 cm/1 inch piece of fresh root ginger
1 small leek
1.5 ml/1/4 teaspoon dried shrimp paste (terasi)
45 ml/3 tablespoons vegetable oil
1.5–2.5 ml/1/4–1/2 teaspoon sambal ulek
30 ml/2 tablespoons soy sauce
15 ml/1 tablespoon palm sugar
rice, to serve

Approximately per portion:
2,100 kJ/500 kcal
27 g protein, 41 g fat
8 g carbohydrate

● Approximate preparation time: 30 minutes

---

1. With a sharp knife, make cross-cuts in the base of the tomatoes and briefly blanch them in boiling water. Drain and when cool enough to handle, peel, seed and finely dice the flesh.

2. Mix together the tamarind pulp and warm water, then press the mixture through a strainer, reserving the juice. Discard the pulp in the strainer.

3. Cut the pork into small pieces. Thinly slice the onion and crush the garlic. Finely grate the ginger. Thinly slice the leek. Mash the shrimp paste.

4. Heat the vegetable oil in a preheated wok. Add the pork, onion, garlic and ginger and stir-fry over a high heat for 3 minutes. Reduce the heat and add the sambal ulek, soy sauce and palm sugar. Simmer over a low heat for 10–15 minutes. Serve with rice.

Pork in soy sauce

Babi kecap

Easy

Serves 4
600 g/1 lb 5 oz pork fillet
3 cloves garlic
2.5 cm/1 inch piece of fresh root ginger
1.5–2.5 ml/1/4–1/2 teaspoon sambal ulek
1 bunch spring onions
1 red pepper
45 ml/3 tablespoons vegetable oil
75 ml/5 tablespoons sweet soy sauce (kecap manis)
10 ml/2 teaspoons palm sugar
105 ml/7 tablespoons water
15 ml/1 tablespoon grated coconut

Approximately per portion:
2,200 kJ/520 kcal
28 g protein, 41 g fat
10 g carbohydrate

● Approximate preparation time: 1 hour 20 minutes of which 1 hour is marinating time

---

1. Slice the pork and then cut it into 4 cm/1 1/2 inch strips. Crush the garlic and finely grate the root ginger.

2. Put the pork, garlic and ginger into a bowl and mix in the sambal ulek. Cover and set aside to marinate for at least 1 hour.

3. Cut the green parts of the spring onions into 4 cm/1 1/2 inch strips and thinly slice the white parts into rings. Core and seed the red pepper and cut the flesh into thin strips.

4. Heat the vegetable oil in a preheated wok. Add the pork, together with the marinade, the spring onions and red pepper and stir-fry over a high heat for about 5 minutes.

5. Reduce the heat, add the sweet soy sauce, palm sugar and water and simmer over a low heat for about 10 minutes, until the sauce has thickened. Serve immediately sprinkled with grated coconut.

Above: Sweet-and-sour pork
Below: Pork in soy sauce

Braised beef

Rendang daging

Famous recipe

Serves 4
15 ml/1 tablespoon tamarind pulp
250 ml/8 fl oz warm water
750g/1 lb 10 oz braising steak
1 large onion
3 cloves garlic
2.5 cm/1 inch piece of fresh
    root ginger
1.5 ml/¼ teaspoon dried shrimp
    paste (terasi)
75 ml/5 tablespoons vegetable oil
2.5–5 ml/½–1 teaspoon sambal
    ulek
5 ml/1 teaspoon ground cumin
5 ml/1 teaspoon ground coriander
2.5 ml/½ teaspoon ground turmeric
15 ml/1 tablespoon palm sugar
400 ml/14 fl oz coconut milk
salt
rice or Indonesian flat bread,
    to serve

Approximately per portion:
1,700 kJ/400 kcal
40 g protein, 24 g fat
7 g carbohydrate

● Approximate preparation
  time: 1 hour 20 minutes

---

1. Mash the tamarind pulp in the warm water and press it through a strainer, reserving the juice. Discard the pulp.

2. Dice the braising steak. Finely dice the onion and crush the garlic. Finely grate the ginger. Mash the shrimp paste with the back of a small spoon.

3. Heat the vegetable oil in a saucepan. Add the meat, onion, ginger and garlic and stir-fry over a high heat. Add the sambal ulek, cumin, coriander, turmeric, palm sugar and salt to taste and stir-fry until the meat is browned all over.

4. Pour in the tamarind juice and the coconut milk. Bring to the boil, reduce the heat, cover and braise over a low heat for about 1 hour. Serve hot or cold with rice or Indonesian flat bread.

Beef with Chinese chives

Sambal goreng daging

Chinese chives are also known as garlic chives or flowering chives.

Quick

Serves 3
500 g/1¼ lb beef fillet
2 fresh red chillies, each about
    10 cm/4 inches long
2.5 cm/1 inch piece of fresh
    root ginger
3 cloves garlic
200 g/7 oz Chinese chives or
    1 bunch spring onions
45 ml/3 tablespoons vegetable oil
45 ml/3 tablespoons lemon juice
30 ml/2 tablespoons soy sauce
rice, to serve

Approximately per portion:
1,300 kJ/310 kcal
36 g protein, 16 g fat
4 g carbohydrate

● Approximate preparation
  time: 20 minutes

---

1. Cut the meat into thin strips. Seed the chillies and cut them into thin strips. Finely grate the ginger and crush the garlic.

2. Trim the Chinese chives, if using. Cut the green parts of the spring onions, if using, into 4 cm/1½ inch pieces and thinly slice the white parts into rings.

3. Heat the vegetable oil in a preheated wok or a large frying pan. Add the beef, chillies, ginger and garlic and stir-fry over a high heat for about 5 minutes.

4. Add the Chinese chives or spring onions, lemon juice and soy sauce and cook over a medium heat for a further 3 minutes. Serve immediately with rice.

Tip

Even the tiniest amount of the volatile oils from the chilli on your hands or in your eyes burns horribly, so be sure to wear disposable gloves.

Above: Braised beef
Below: Beef with Chinese chives

Crispy chicken legs

Ayam goreng

Economical • Easy

Serves 4
8 chicken legs
4 cloves garlic
about 2 cm/^{3}/$_4$ inch piece of
   galangal or fresh root ginger
30 ml/2 tablespoons soy sauce
45 ml/3 tablespoons sweet soy
   sauce (kecap manis)
15 ml/1 tablespoon palm sugar
7.5 ml/1^1/$_2$ teaspoons freshly ground
   black pepper

Approximately per portion:
1,500 kJ/360 kcal
63 g protein, 9 g fat
7 g carbohydrate

● Approximate preparation
   time: 40 minutes

---

1. Arrange the chicken legs in a single layer in a roasting tin or ovenproof dish. Crush the garlic and finely grate the galangal or ginger. Mix together the garlic, galangal or ginger, soy sauce, sweet soy sauce, palm sugar and pepper. Spread the spice mixture evenly over the chicken legs.

2. Roast the chicken legs in a preheated oven at 180°C/350°F/Gas 4, turning them occasionally, for about 30 minutes. Test to see if they are cooked by inserting the point of a sharp knife in the thickest part. If the juices run clear, the chicken is ready.

Chicken curry Javanese style

Ayam kari jawa

Exclusive • For guests

Serves 4
1 medium chicken
3 onions
3 cloves garlic
2.5 cm/1 inch piece of fresh
   root ginger
3 stalks of lemon grass
12 macadamia nuts
3 cloves
2.5 ml/^{1}/$_2$ teaspoon sambal ulek
5 ml/1 teaspoon ground coriander
2.5 ml/^{1}/$_2$ teaspoon grated nutmeg
15 ml/1 tablespoon palm sugar
90 ml/6 tablespoons vegetable oil
400 ml/14 fl oz coconut milk
1 cinnamon stick
45 ml/3 tablespoons freshly grated
   coconut or desiccated coconut
salt
rice, to serve

Approximately per portion:
2,800 kJ/ 670 kcal
47 g protein, 45 g fat
21 g carbohydrate

● Approximate preparation
   time: 1^1/$_2$ hours

---

1. Cut off the chicken legs and wings with poultry shears. Cut the chicken body in half along the breastbone. Cut each half into two pieces.

2. Finely dice the onions and crush the garlic. Finely grate the ginger. Cut the lower thick part of the lemon grass into wafer-thin slices. Finely grate the macadamia nuts. Pound the cloves in a mortar with a pestle.

3. Mix together the onions, garlic, ginger, lemon grass, nuts, cloves, sambal ulek, coriander, nutmeg, palm sugar, 30 ml/2 tablespoons of the vegetable oil and salt to taste.

4. Heat the remaining vegetable oil in a large saucepan. Add the chicken pieces and fry on all sides over a medium heat. Reduce the heat, add the spice paste and fry, stirring constantly, for 3 minutes.

5. Add the coconut milk and the cinnamon stick, cover and simmer over a low heat for about 30 minutes.

6. Remove and discard the cinnamon stick. Stir in the grated coconut and serve the curry immediately with rice.

Above: Chicken curry Javanese style
Below: Crispy chicken legs

Fish Balinese style

Ikan Bali

This dish is delicious made with any white fish fillets.

Quick

Serves 4
15 ml/1 tablespoon tamarind pulp
150 ml/1/4 pint warm water
2 medium onions
2.5 cm/1 inch piece of fresh
*   root ginger*
3 stalks of lemon grass
120 ml/4 fl oz vegetable oil
1.5–2.5 ml/1/4–1/2 teaspoon sambal
*   ulek*
10 ml/2 teaspoons palm sugar
2.5 ml/1/2 teaspoon laos powder
30 ml/2 tablespoons sweet soy
*   sauce (kecap manis)*
1 kg/2 1/4 lb white fish fillets, such as
*   cod or haddock*
5 ml/1 teaspoon salt
rice, to serve

Approximately per portion:
1,400 kJ/330 kcal
38 g protein, 18 g fat
6 g carbohydrate

● Approximate preparation
   time: 35 minutes

1. Mash the tamarind pulp in the warm water, press it through a strainer and reserve the liquid. Discard the pulp.

2. Finely dice the onions. Finely grate the ginger. Thinly slice the lower part of the lemon grass.

3. Heat 30 ml/2 tablespoons of the vegetable oil in a frying pan. Add the onions, ginger and lemon grass and fry over a medium heat, stirring frequently, until the onions are lightly golden brown.

4. Pour in the tamarind juice. Add the sambal ulek, palm sugar, laos powder and sweet soy sauce. Simmer over a low heat for about 10 minutes, or until thickened.

5. Cut the fish into 2 cm/3/4 inch thick slices and rub it with the salt. Heat the remaining vegetable oil in a frying pan. Add the fish and fry on both sides over a medium heat for about 5 minutes. Transfer the fish to a serving dish, cover with the sauce and serve with rice.

Sea bream in coconut sauce

Ikan panggang santen

Sea bream is a large family of fish, ranging in colour from black to red.

Exquisite

Serves 4
4 x 400 g/14 oz sea bream, scaled,
*   cleaned, gutted and trimmed*
2 onions
2 cloves garlic
2 fresh red chillies, each about
*   10 cm/4 inches long*
1/2 bunch fresh coriander
750 ml/1 1/4 pints oil, for deep-frying
45 ml/3 tablespoons vegetable oil
400 ml/14 fl oz coconut milk
juice of 1/2 lemon
10 ml/2 teaspoons palm sugar
30 ml/2 tablespoons grated coconut
salt

Approximately per portion:
2,400 kJ/570 kcal
43 g protein, 40 g fat
12 g carbohydrate

● Approximate preparation
   time: 1 hour

1. With a sharp knife, make small incisions about 1 cm/1/2 inch apart on both sides of the fish. Season the bream with salt inside and out.

2. Finely chop the onions and the garlic. Seed the chillies and cut the flesh into thin strips. Reserve a few coriander leaves for the garnish and finely chop the remainder.

3. Heat the oil for deep-frying in a large saucepan or deep-fryer. Add the bream and fry over a medium heat for about 10 minutes. Drain them thoroughly on kitchen paper.

4. Heat the vegetable oil in a large frying pan. Add the onions, garlic and chillies and fry, stirring frequently, until the onions are lightly browned. Pour in the coconut milk and lemon juice. Add two thirds of the chopped coriander and the palm sugar. Lay the bream in the sauce and simmer over a low heat for about 10 minutes.

5. Transfer the fish and sauce to a warm serving dish, sprinkle with the remaining chopped coriander and the grated coconut, garnish with the reserved coriander leaves and serve immediately.

Above: Fish Balinese style
Below: Sea bream in coconut sauce

Red mullet in banana leaf parcels

Ikan isi

For guests

Serves 4
1 banana leaf
4 red mullet, cleaned
1 medium onion
2.5 cm/1 inch piece of fresh
*   root ginger*
2 cloves garlic
25 ml/1½ tablespoons vegetable oil
45 ml/3 tablespoons sweet soy
*   sauce (kecap manis)*
juice of 1 lemon
1.5 ml/¼ teaspoon ground
*   cinnamon*
1.5 ml/¼ teaspoon ground cloves
1.5 ml/¼ teaspoon ground turmeric
2.5 ml/½ teaspoon ground cumin
10 ml/2 teaspoons ground coriander
freshly ground black pepper

Approximately per portion:
1,500 kJ/360 kcal
59 g protein, 12 g fat
3 g carbohydrate

● Approximate preparation
   time: 1 hour

1. Thaw the banana leaf, if necessary, and blanch briefly, if wished. Using a sharp knife or scissors, cut it into 4 squares measuring about 30–40 cm/ 12–16 inches. Make small incisions about 1 cm/½ inch apart on the outer skin on both sides of the red mullet.

2. Finely dice the onion and ginger and crush the garlic. Mix together the onion, garlic, ginger, vegetable oil, sweet soy sauce, lemon juice, cinnamon, cloves, turmeric, cumin, coriander and pepper to taste.

3. Stuff the fish with the spice paste and spread the remaining paste on the outside. Wrap each fish in a separate piece of prepared banana leaf and secure with cocktail sticks.

4. Place the fish parcels in a single layer in a roasting tin. Bake them in a preheated oven at 200°C/400°F/ Gas 6 for about 40 minutes. Serve the fish parcels still fastened and unwrap them at the table.

Seafood in batter

Ikan goreng

Rather expensive

Serves 4
200 g/7 oz salmon or tuna fish fillet
200 g/7 oz cod fillet
200 g/7 oz raw, peeled tiger
  prawns, deveined
200 g/7 oz small prepared squid
200 g/7 oz shelled mussels
750 ml/1 1/4 pints vegetable oil, for
  deep-frying
juice of 1 lemon
For the batter:
75 g/3 oz plain flour
45 ml/3 tablespoons cornflour
5 ml/1 teaspoon baking powder
15 ml/1 tablespoon vegetable oil
salt

Approximately per portion:
2,100 kJ/500 kcal
42 g protein, 27 g fat
21 g carbohydrate

● Approximate preparation
  time: 50 minutes

Tip

You can marinate the seafood in
lemon or tamarind juice for
about 6 hours before frying.

1. Cut the salmon or tuna and cod fillets into 2.5 cm/1 inch chunks.

2. To make the batter, mix together the flour, cornflour, baking powder and a pinch of salt in a bowl. Add the vegetable oil and a little hot water and stir into a smooth, thin batter. Dip the fish chunks and seafood in the batter.

3. Heat the oil for deep-frying in a large saucepan or a deep-fryer. Lower a few of the fish chunks and seafood into the hot oil and fry them for 3–5 minutes, until they are golden brown. Do not add too many at a time to prevent them from sticking together.

4. Remove the fried fish and seafood with a slotted spoon and drain them on kitchen paper. Transfer to a warm serving dish, sprinkle with lemon juice and serve immediately.

Squid Borneo style

Cumi cumi kalimantan

Quick

Serves 4
1 squid, ready to cook, about
    800 g–1 kg/1³/4–2¹/4 lb
15 ml/1 tablespoon tamarind pulp
150 ml/¹/4 pint warm water
45 ml/3 tablespoons vegetable oil
1.5–2.5 ml/¹/4–¹/2 teaspoon sambal
    ulek
30 ml/2 tablespoons sweet soy
    sauce (kecap manis)
salt

Approximately per portion:
950 kJ/230 kcal
39 g protein, 8 g fat
0 g carbohydrate

● Approximate preparation
   time: 25 minutes

---

1. Using a sharp knife, cut the squid into bite-size pieces. Mash the tamarind pulp in the warm water and press it through a strainer, reserving the liquid. Discard the pulp.

2. Heat the vegetable oil in a preheated wok or a large frying pan. Add the squid and the sambal ulek and stir-fry until the squid begins to brown.

3. Add the tamarind juice and sweet soy sauce and season to taste with salt. Simmer over a medium heat, stirring occasionally, until the sauce is well thickened. Serve warm or cold.

Dried shrimp with egg

Udang goreng telur

Easy • Quick

Serves 2
30 ml/2 tablespoons dried shrimp
1 medium onion
2 cloves garlic
2.5 cm/1 inch piece of fresh
    root ginger
5 macadamia nuts
4 eggs
30 ml/2 tablespoons vegetable oil
¹/2 bunch fresh coriander or flat
    leaf parsley

Approximately per portion:
1,000 kJ/240 kcal
14 g protein, 18 g fat
5 g carbohydrate

● Approximate preparation
   time: 25 minutes

---

1. Rinse the dried shrimp in a strainer and drain well. Finely dice the onion and crush the garlic. Finely grate the ginger and macadamia nuts. Beat the eggs. Finely chop the coriander or parsley.

2. Heat the vegetable oil in a preheated wok or a large, heavy-based frying pan. Add the shrimp, onion, garlic, root ginger and macadamia nuts and fry over a medium heat, stirring frequently, until the onion is browned.

3. Pour the eggs evenly over the mixture and cook over a medium heat for 3–5 minutes. When the top has set, carefully turn the omelette over and fry the other side until golden brown.

4. Slide the omelette out of the wok or pan on to a plate. Cut it in half, sprinkle with the coriander or parsley and serve.

Above: Squid Borneo style
Below: Dried shrimp with egg

Fried mixed vegetables

Cap cay goreng

Easy

Serves 4
200 g/7 oz skinless, boneless
   chicken breasts
1 small onion
2 cloves garlic
2.5 cm/1 inch piece of fresh
   root ginger
115 g/4 oz green beans
250 g/9 oz Chinese leaves
1 carrot
200 g/7 oz can bamboo shoots
115 g/4 oz fresh beansprouts
30 ml/2 tablespoons vegetable oil
1.5–2.5 ml/^{1}/4–^{1}/2 teaspoon sambal
   ulek
250 ml/8 fl oz water
10 ml/2 teaspoons cornflour
30 ml/2 tablespoons peeled
   raw prawns
45 ml/3 tablespoons soy sauce

Approximately per portion:
720 kJ/170 kcal
19 g protein, 6 g fat
12 g carbohydrate

● Approximate preparation
   time: 40 minutes

1. Cut the chicken into very thin strips. Finely chop the onion, garlic and ginger. Cut the beans into 5 cm/2 inch long pieces.

2. Cut the Chinese leaves into bite-size pieces. Coarsely grate the carrot. Drain and rinse the bamboo shoots. Rinse the beansprouts and drain them.

3. Heat the vegetable oil in a preheated wok. Add the chicken, onion, garlic, ginger, beans and sambal ulek and stir-fry for about 5 minutes. Add 200 ml/7 fl oz of the water and the prawns. Bring to the boil over a medium heat and cook until about half the water has evaporated.

4. Add the Chinese leaves, carrot, bamboo shoots and beansprouts and stir to mix. Cover and simmer over a low heat for 5 minutes.

5. Mix the cornflour with the remaining water to make a smooth paste. Stir the paste into the wok, together with the soy sauce, and cook, stirring constantly, until thickened. Serve immediately.

Vegetable bites

Pergedel sayur

Economical

Serves 4 (makes 30–40)
1 large carrot
115 g/4 oz celery
1 small leek
200 g/7 oz Chinese leaves
200 g/7 oz skinless, boneless
   chicken breasts
1 onion
2 cloves garlic
2.5 cm/1 inch piece of fresh
   root ginger
200 g/7 oz fresh beansprouts
2.5 ml/^{1}/2 teaspoon sambal ulek
10 ml/2 teaspoons ground coriander
1 egg
about 90 ml/6 tablespoons plain
   flour
750 ml/1^1/4 pints oil, for deep-frying
salt

**For 40 bites,
approximately per bite:**
140 kJ/33 kcal
2 g protein, 2 g fat
2 g carbohydrate

● Approximate preparation
   time: 45 minutes

1. Finely chop the carrot and celery. Cut the leek into quarters lengthways and then cut it across into thin strips. Finely chop the Chinese leaves. Cut the chicken into thin strips about 2 cm/^{3}/4 inch long. Finely chop the onion, garlic and ginger.

2. Mix together the carrot, celery, leek, Chinese leaves, chicken, onion, garlic, ginger and beansprouts in a bowl. Add the sambal ulek, coriander, egg, flour and salt to taste. Thoroughly combine to make a soft mixture.

3. Take 7.5 ml/1^1/2 teaspoons of the mixture at a time and shape it into a small walnut-size bites. Dry them on kitchen paper.

4. Heat the oil for deep-frying in a large saucepan or deep-fryer. Add the bites, a few at a time, and fry for 3–4 minutes, until they are golden brown. Remove with a slotted spoon and drain on kitchen paper while you cook the remainder. Serve immediately.

Above: Fried mixed vegetables
Below: Vegetable bites

Spinach soup with prawns

Sayur bayam

Quick • Easy

Serves 4
500 g/1 1/4 lb young spinach
1 medium-size sweet potato or
  1 potato
1 onion
2 cloves garlic
2.5 cm/1 inch piece of fresh
  root ginger
30 ml/2 tablespoons vegetable oil
330 g/11 1/2 oz can sweetcorn
  kernels
115 g/4 oz peeled raw prawns
200 ml/7 fl oz water
400 ml/14 fl oz coconut milk
1.5–2.5 ml/1/4–1/2 teaspoon sambal
  ulek
5 ml/1 teaspoon ground coriander
salt

Approximately per portion:
1,600 kJ/380 kcal
16 g protein, 8 g fat
61 g carbohydrate

● Approximate preparation
  time: 25 minutes

---

1. Coarsely chop the spinach, removing any tough stalks. Peel and finely dice the sweet potato or potato. Finely chop the onion, garlic and ginger.

2. Heat the vegetable oil in a large saucepan. Add the onion, garlic, ginger and sweet potato or potato and fry over a low heat, stirring frequently, until the onion is soft and translucent.

3. Add the spinach and cook until the leaves wilt. Stir in the sweetcorn, together with the can juices. Add the prawns, water and coconut milk. Season with the sambal ulek, coriander and salt to taste. Bring to the boil, cover, reduce the heat and simmer for 10 minutes. Serve immediately.

Vegetable soup

Sayur lodeh

Exquisite

Serves 4
250 g/9 oz cauliflower or broccoli
1 bunch spring onions
1 large floury potato
1 small courgette
1 small leek
115 g/4 oz white cabbage leaves
3 cloves garlic
2.5 ml/1/2 teaspoon dried shrimp
    paste (terasi)
30 ml/2 tablespoons vegetable oil
1.5–2.5 ml/1/4–1/2 teaspoon sambal
    ulek
750 ml/1 1/4 pints coconut milk
200 ml/7 fl oz water
115 g/4 oz spinach
10 ml/2 teaspoons palm sugar
30 ml/2 tablespoons soy sauce
45 ml/3 tablespoons canned
    sweetcorn kernels
salt and freshly ground black pepper
sweet soy sauce (kecap manis)

Approximately per portion:
760 kJ/180 kcal
7 g protein, 6 g fat
26 g carbohydrate

● Approximate preparation
  time: 45 minutes

---

1. Divide the cauliflower or broccoli into florets. Cut the spring onions into 4 cm/1 1/2 inch long pieces. Dice the potato into 1 cm/1/2 inch cubes. Slice the courgette. Slice the leek into rings. Cut the white cabbage into bite-size pieces. Crush the garlic. Mash the shrimp paste with the back of a spoon.

2. Heat the vegetable oil in a large saucepan. Add the spring onions, garlic, shrimp paste and sambal ulek and fry over a low heat, stirring constantly, for about 3 minutes. Stir in the coconut milk and water.

3. Add the cauliflower or broccoli, spring onions, potato, courgette, leek, cabbage, spinach, palm sugar and soy sauce. Bring to the boil, cover and cook over a medium heat for about 10 minutes.

4. Add the sweetcorn. Season the soup with salt, pepper and sweet soy sauce and serve immediately.

Above: Vegetable soup
Below: Spinach soup with prawns

Broccoli with coconut sauce

Brokoli bumbu kelapa

Exquisite

Serves 2–3
500 g/1¼ lb broccoli
1 small onion
1 clove garlic
30 ml/2 tablespoons vegetable oil
115 g/4 oz freshly grated coconut or
  desiccated coconut
1.5 ml/¼ teaspoon sambal ulek
75 ml/5 tablespoons water
juice of 1 lemon
5 ml/1 teaspoon laos powder
salt

For 3 portions
approximately per portion:
1,027 kJ/ 240 kcal
7 g protein, 12 g fat
28 g carbohydrate

● Approximate preparation
  time: 20 minutes

---

1. Divide the broccoli into florets. Put them into a saucepan and add a pinch of salt and enough water to reach about 2 cm/³/₄ inch up the side of the pan. Cover, bring to the boil and cook over a medium heat for 10–15 minutes, until tender, but still firm to the bite.

2. Finely dice the onion and crush the garlic. Heat the vegetable oil in a frying pan. Add the coconut, onion, garlic and the sambal ulek and fry over a medium heat, stirring frequently, until the coconut begins to brown.

3. Add the water and lemon juice and season with the laos powder and salt to taste.

4. Thoroughly drain the broccoli and divide it between 2 or 3 warm individual serving plates. Serve immediately, together with the coconut sauce.

Tofu with sweet potatoes

Sambal goreng tahu

Can be prepared in advance

Serves 4
450 g/1 lb tofu
500 g/1¼ lb sweet potatoes
  or potatoes
1 small tomato
½ bunch spring onions
3 cloves garlic
750 ml/1¼ pints oil, for
  deep-frying
30 ml/2 tablespoons vegetable oil
2.5 ml/½ teaspoon sambal ulek
115 g/4 oz shelled peanuts
30 ml/2 tablespoons soy sauce
juice of ½ lemon
50 ml/2 fl oz water
30 ml/2 tablespoons palm sugar
5 ml/1 teaspoon ground
  coriander
2.5 ml/½ teaspoon laos powder
30 ml/2 tablespoons sweet soy
  sauce (kecap manis)

Approximately per portion:
2,600 kJ/620 kcal
17 g protein, 46 g fat
35 g carbohydrate

● Approximate preparation
  time: 45 minutes

---

1. Wipe the tofu dry and cut it into 1 cm/½ inch cubes. Peel the sweet potatoes or potatoes and cut them into 1 cm/½ inch cubes. Finely dice the tomato. Thinly slice the spring onions into rings. Crush the garlic.

2. Heat the oil for deep-frying in a large saucepan or a deep-fryer. Add the tofu and fry for about 3–5 minutes, until crisp. Remove the tofu with a slotted and drain it on kitchen paper.

3. Meanwhile, add the potatoes to the hot oil and fry until crisp. Remove them with a slotted spoon and drain on kitchen paper.

4. Heat the vegetable oil in a preheated wok or frying pan. Add the spring onions, garlic, sambal ulek and peanuts and stir-fry over a medium heat.

5. Add the tomato, soy sauce, lemon juice and water. Simmer over a low heat for 2 minutes. Add the tofu and potatoes and season with the palm sugar, coriander, laos powder and sweet soy sauce. Serve immediately.

Above: Broccoli with coconut sauce
Below: Tofu with sweet potatoes

Crispy tofu balls

Tahu bola

Rather time-consuming

Serves 4 (makes 20)
450 g/1 lb tofu
1 medium onion
2 cloves garlic
2.5 cm/1 inch piece of fresh
    root ginger
1.5 ml/^{1}/4 teaspoon sambal ulek
30 ml/2 tablespoons grated coconut
2 eggs
750 ml/1 ^{1}/4 pints oil, for deep-frying
salt
coriander sprigs and tomato wedges,
    to garnish

Approximately per portion:
1,450 kJ/345 kcal
10 g protein, 30 g fat
10 g carbohydrate

● Approximate preparation
  time: 2^1/2 hours of which
  2 hours are standing time

---

1. Wipe the tofu dry and mash it with a fork. Finely dice the onion and crush the garlic. Finely grate the root ginger.

2. Mix together the tofu, onion, garlic, ginger, sambal ulek, grated coconut and salt to taste. Set aside for about 2 hours.

3. Heat the oil for deep-frying in a large saucepan or in a deep-fryer. Mix the eggs into the tofu mixture.

4. Take out 7.5 ml/1 ^{1}/2 teaspoons of the mixture at a time and form it into a ball. Wipe the balls dry with kitchen paper. Add them, a few at a time, to the hot oil and fry until crisp. Remove with a slotted spoon and drain thoroughly on kitchen paper.

5. Transfer the tofu balls to a serving dish, garnish with coriander sprigs and tomato wedges and serve immediately.

Tofu, tempeh and potatoes

Tahu, tempe, kentang goreng

Easy

Serves 4
450 g/1 lb tofu
450 g/1 lb tempeh
500 g/1 ^{1}/4 lb potatoes
For the marinade:
1 small onion
6–8 cloves garlic
5 ml/1 teaspoon laos powder
5 ml/1 teaspoon ground coriander
2.5 ml/^{1}/2 teaspoon sambal ulek
30 ml/2 tablespoons palm sugar
60 ml/4 tablespoons soy sauce
200 ml/7 fl oz warm water
750 ml/1 ^{1}/4 pints oil, for
    deep-frying

Approximately per portion:
2,100 kJ/500 kcal
19 g protein, 34 g fat
30 g carbohydrate

● Marinating time: 6 hours
● Approximate preparation
  time: 40 minutes

---

1. Wipe dry the tofu and the tempeh with kitchen paper. Cut them in half lengthways and then into thin slices. Peel and thinly slice the potatoes.

2. To make the marinade, finely dice the onion and crush the garlic. Mix the onion and garlic with the laos powder, coriander, sambal ulek, palm sugar, soy sauce and warm water in a shallow dish.

3. Add the tofu, tempeh and potatoes to the marinade and set aside to marinate for at least 6 hours.

4. Remove the tofu, tempeh and potato slices from the marinade and drain. Heat the oil for deep-frying in a large saucepan or a deep-fryer. Fry the tofu, tempeh and potato slices in it, a few at a time, for about 5 minutes, until they are crispy. Remove the slices and drain them on kitchen paper. Serve hot.

Above: Crispy tofu balls
Below: Tofu, tempeh and potatoes

Tempeh in black sauce

Tempe goreng kecap

Easy

Serves 2–3
1 onion
3 cloves garlic
450 g/1 lb tempeh
150 ml/$1^{1}/4$ pint vegetable oil
2.5 ml/$^{1}/2$ teaspoon sambal ulek
10 ml/2 teaspoons palm sugar
30 ml/2 tablespoons soy sauce
75 ml/5 tablespoons sweet soy
    sauce (kecap manis)

Approximately per portion:
1,900 kJ/440 kcal
12 g protein, 40 g fat
11 g carbohydrate

● Approximate preparation
   time: 30 minutes

---

1. Finely chop the onion and garlic. Wipe the tempeh dry on kitchen paper, cut it in half lengthways and then into slices.

2. Heat the vegetable oil in a large, heavy-based frying pan. Add the tempeh slices and fry on both sides over a medium heat. Remove from the pan and drain thoroughly on kitchen paper.

3. Carefully pour off all but 30 ml/ 2 tablespoons of the oil and return the pan to the heat. Add the onion, garlic and sambal ulek and fry over a medium heat, stirring occasionally, until the onions are lightly browned.

4. Add the tempeh slices. Season with the palm sugar, soy sauce and sweet soy sauce. Stir carefully and simmer over a low heat until the sauce has thickened. Transfer to a serving dish and serve immediately.

Noodle soup with tofu

Kari mie tahu

Exquisite

Serves 4
1 small leek
1 onion
3 cloves garlic
2.5 cm/1 inch piece of fresh
   root ginger
3 stalks of lemon grass
8 macadamia nuts
2.5 ml/$^{1}/2$ teaspoon dried shrimp
   paste (terasi)
120 ml/4 fl oz vegetable oil
2.5–5 ml/$^{1}/2$–1 teaspoon sambal
   ulek
750 ml/$1^{1}/4$ pints chicken or
   vegetable stock
200 ml/7 fl oz coconut milk
15 ml/1 tablespoon ground
   coriander
250 g/9 oz egg noodles
45 ml/3 tablespoons soy sauce
450 g/1 lb tofu
200 g/7 oz fresh beansprouts
45 ml/3 tablespoons sweet soy
   sauce (kecap manis)

Approximately per portion:
2,700 kJ/640 kcal
24 g protein, 36 g fat
53 g carbohydrate

● Approximate preparation
   time: 40 minutes

---

1. Thinly slice the leek into rings. Finely chop the onion, garlic and ginger. Cut the thick lower part of the lemon grass into wafer-thin slices. Finely grate the macadamia nuts. Mash the shrimp paste with the back of a spoon.

2. Heat 30 ml/2 tablespoons of the vegetable oil in a large saucepan. Add the onion, garlic, ginger, lemon grass, nuts, shrimp paste and sambal ulek and fry over a medium heat, stirring frequently, until the onion is lightly browned.

3. Add the chicken or vegetable stock and coconut milk and bring to the boil. Add the leek, coriander, noodles and soy sauce, cover and cook over a medium heat until the noodles are soft.

4. Heat the remaining vegetable oil in a frying pan. Wipe the tofu dry with kitchen paper, cut it in half lengthways and then into slices. Add it to the pan and fry on both sides until crispy. Remove from the pan with a slotted spoon and drain on kitchen paper.

5. When the noodles are tender, remove the saucepan from the heat. Stir in the tofu, the beansprouts and sweet soy sauce. Set aside, covered, for 10 minutes before serving.

Above: Tempeh in black sauce
Below: Noodle soup with tofu

Prawn crackers

Krupuk

These light-as-air crisps are made from ground prawns and tapioca starch. You can buy them ready-to-fry or ready-fried in Chinese supermarkets and Asian shops.

Quick

Serves 4
20 small or 4 large prawn crackers
750 ml/1 1/4 pints oil, for deep-frying

Approximately per portion:
894 kJ/214 kcal
1 g protein, 18 g fat
10 g carbohydrate

● Approximate preparation
  time: 15 minutes
---

1. Heat the oil for deep-frying in a large saucepan or a deep-fryer. It must be hot enough to enable the crackers to rise quickly, but not so hot that they turn brown. It is best to test with a small piece.

2. Fry the crackers in the vegetable oil, but do not let them go brown. Fry only a few crackers at a time, as they double in size when fried. As soon as the crackers have risen to the surface, remove them from the pan with a slotted spoon. Drain well on kitchen paper.

Stuffed rice rolls

Lemper ketan

Serve these rolls with various hot sauces – sambals – which you can obtain ready-made from Chinese supermarkets or make yourself (see Tip).

Can be prepared in advance

Serves 4 (Makes 20)
1 banana leaf
200 g/7 oz sticky rice (ketan)
400 ml/14 fl oz coconut milk
400 ml/14 fl oz water
1/2 bunch spring onions
500 g/1 1/4 lb veal
30 ml/2 tablespoons vegetable oil
2.5 ml/1/2 teaspoon sambal ulek
30 ml/2 tablespoons soy sauce
45 ml/3 tablespoons sweet soy
  sauce (kecap manis)
salt

Approximately per portion:
7,000 kJ/1,650 kcal
155 g protein, 35 g fat
210 g carbohydrate

● Approximate preparation
  time: 1 hour
---

1. Thaw the banana leaf, if necessary, and blanch, if wished. Using kitchen scissors or a sharp knife cut it into 20 rectangles measuring 10 × 15 cm/ 4 × 6 inches. Otherwise use aluminium foil.

2. Rinse the sticky rice in a strainer and drain it. Put it into a saucepan with a close-fitting lid, together with 300 ml/1/2 pint of the coconut milk and the water. Bring to the boil, reduce the heat,

cover and cook over a low heat for about 15 minutes.

3. Meanwhile, thinly slice the spring onions into rings. Cut the veal into thin strips 2 cm/3/4 inch long. Heat the vegetable oil in a frying pan. Add the meat, spring onions and sambal ulek and fry, stirring frequently, for about 3 minutes.

4. Add the remaining coconut milk, the soy sauce and sweet soy sauce. Simmer over a medium heat until thickened, then remove the pan from the heat.

5. Divide the rice and meat mixture between the banana leaf rectangles. Roll them up and fasten the ends with half a cocktail stick. Serve the rolls cold or warm them through by steaming them for 15 minutes.

Tip

To make sambal tomaat, peel and quarter 400 g/14 oz beefsteak tomatoes and put them in a food processor. Add 1 fresh red chilli, halved and seeded, if liked, 2 cloves garlic, 115 g/4 oz brown sugar and a pinch of salt and process to form a purée. Heat 45 ml/ 3 tablespoons vegetable oil in a heavy-based frying pan. Add the purée and fry, stirring constantly, until thick. Stir in 15 ml/ 1 tablespoon lemon juice and set aside to cool.

Above: Stuffed rice rolls
Below: Prawn crackers

Prawn balls

Rempah udang

Easy

Serves 4 (makes 24)
250 g/9 oz peeled raw prawns
200 g/7 oz fresh beansprouts
1 bunch spring onions
2.5 cm/1 inch piece of fresh
    root ginger
1 egg
115 g/4 oz plain flour
5 ml/1 teaspoon baking powder
2.5 ml/¹/₂ teaspoon sambal ulek
750 ml/1¹/₄ pints oil, for deep-frying
salt

Approximately per portion:
1,740 kJ/414 kcal
18 g protein, 30 g fat
18 g carbohydrate

● Approximate preparation
  time: 40 minutes

---

1. Put the prawns, beansprouts, spring onions and ginger into a food processor and process until very finely chopped. Transfer the mixture to a bowl.

2. Add the egg, flour, baking powder, sambal ulek and salt to taste and knead to a firm, workable dough. If the dough is too stiff, add lukewarm water, a spoonful at a time.

3. Heat the oil for deep-frying in a large, heavy-based frying pan or a deep-fryer.

4. Take 7.5 ml/1¹/₂ teaspoons of the dough at a time and form it into a walnut-size ball. Carefully drop the balls, a few at a time, into the hot oil and fry them until crispy. Remove the prawn balls with a slotted spoon and drain thoroughly on kitchen paper. If serving hot, keep warm while you cook the remainder.

5. Serve the prawn balls hot or cold as a snack or as a side dish to a rice table.

Sweetcorn croquettes

Pergedel jagung

Economical

Serves 4 (makes 16)
275 g/10 oz can sweetcorn kernels
1 medium onion
115 g/4 oz peanuts
2.5 ml/¹/₂ teaspoon sambal ulek
1 egg
115 g/4 oz plain flour
5 ml/1 teaspoon ground coriander
750 ml/1¹/₄ pints oil, for deep-frying
salt

Approximately per portion:
3,000 kJ/720 kcal
16 g protein, 40 g fat
68 g carbohydrate

● Approximate preparation
  time: 30 minutes

---

1. Drain the sweetcorn well. Finely dice the onion. Crush the peanuts in a mortar with a pestle or process briefly in a food processor. Mix together the sweetcorn, onion and peanuts in a bowl.

2. Add the sambal ulek, egg, flour, coriander and salt to taste and knead to a workable dough. If the dough is too stiff, add warm water, a spoonful at a time.

3. Heat the oil for deep-frying in a large saucepan or a deep-fryer.

4. Take 15 ml/1 tablespoon of the dough at a time and form it into a 5 cm/2 inch croquette. Add the croquettes to the hot oil, a few at a time, and fry until crispy. Remove them with a slotted spoon and drain on kitchen paper.

5. Serve the croquettes hot or cold as a snack or as a side dish to a rice table.

Tip

It is important that deep-fried snacks are thoroughly drained on absorbent kitchen paper before serving – whether hot or cold. Otherwise, they will be unpleasantly greasy.

Above: Prawn balls
Below: Sweetcorn croquettes

Filled pasties

Martabak

The recipe for martabak (pronounced mahtabah) was brought to Indonesia by Arab-Indian traders. Martabak vendors can be seen everywhere in the night markets, especially in western Sumatra. It is quite marvellous to watch them artfully spinning the pastry through the air.

Exquisite • For guests

Serves 4
750 ml/1¹/₄ pints oil, for deep-frying
sweet soy sauce (kecap manis),
   to serve
For the pastry:
300 g/11 oz wholemeal flour
1 egg
60 ml/4 tablespoons vegetable oil,
   plus extra for brushing
150 ml/¹/₄ pint warm water
salt
For the filling:
1 medium onion
2 cloves garlic
150 g/5 oz white cabbage leaves
30 ml/2 tablespoons vegetable oil
2.5 ml/¹/₂ teaspoon sambal ulek
150g/5 oz minced beef
1 egg
salt

Approximately per portion:
2,600 kJ/620 kcal
21 g protein, 34 g fat
69 g carbohydrate

● Approximate preparation
  time: 2³/₄ hours of which
  2 hours are resting time

1. To make the pastry, sift the flour into a bowl. Add the egg, vegetable oil and a pinch of salt. Then add the warm water and work the mixture to a soft dough. Thoroughly knead the dough for a few minutes, until it becomes elastic. If it sticks, rub a little vegetable oil on your hands and on the work surface.

2. Form the pastry into a ball. Brush it all over with vegetable oil, wrap in foil and set aside to rest at room temperature for at least 2 hours.

3. Meanwhile, make the filling. Finely dice the onion and crush the garlic. Finely shred the white cabbage leaves.

4. Heat the vegetable oil in a frying pan. Add the onion, garlic and sambal ulek and fry over a low heat, stirring frequently, until the onion is translucent. Add the beef and cabbage, mix well and season with salt to taste. Fry over a medium heat for about 5 minutes.

5. Remove the pan from the heat, transfer the filling to a bowl and set aside to cool slightly, then stir in the egg.

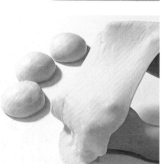

6. Divide the pastry into 4 equal-size pieces and form them into balls. Press the pastry balls flat with the heel of your hand and carefully pull them out to a rectangle 21 × 30 cm/8 × 12 inches, about the size of an A4 sheet of paper. Be careful there are no tears in them. Heat the oil for deep-frying in a large saucepan or a deep-fryer.

7. Put a quarter of the filling into the centre of each of the pastry sheets and fold the pastry over it from the corners to form an envelope. Carefully put the pasties into the hot oil, one at a time, and fry over a low to medium heat until they are crispy.

8. Serve the martabaks warm, together with sweet soy sauce in small bowls.

Green pancakes with coconut filling

Dadar gulung

Exquisite

Serves 4 (makes 12)
115 g/4 oz palm sugar
120 ml/4 fl oz water
200 g/7 oz freshly grated coconut
400 ml/14 fl oz coconut milk
about 10 drops green
    food colouring
4 eggs
300 g/11 oz plain flour
vegetable oil, for frying
salt

Approximately per portion:
3,000 kJ/720 kcal
15 g protein, 21 g fat
117 g carbohydrate

● Approximate preparation
   time: 1 hour

---

1. Put the palm sugar and water into a saucepan and heat gently, stirring constantly, until the sugar has completely dissolved. Add the coconut and simmer over a low heat, stirring constantly, until the liquid has evaporated. Remove the pan from the heat and set aside to cool.

2. Mix the coconut milk with the food colouring. Beat the eggs until light and foamy and add them to the coconut milk. Gradually mix in the flour and a pinch of salt.

3. Heat a little vegetable oil in a small frying pan. Add a ladle of the batter and tilt the pan so that it covers the base. Fry over a medium heat for about 3 minutes. Flip the pancake over with a palette knife or spatula and fry the other side for about 1 minute. Slide it out of the pan and keep warm.

4. Fry 11 more pancakes in the same way, adding more vegetable oil as required.

4. Spread 15 ml/1 tablespoon of the coconut mixture on the bottom edge of each pancake. Fold the outside into the middle and then roll up the pancake from the bottom. Arrange the pancakes on a warm serving dish and serve immediately.

Nut and sesame seed pancakes

Kue apim

Easy

Serves 4 (makes 8)
115 g/4 oz peanuts
45 ml/3 tablespoons sesame seeds
75 ml/5 tablespoons sugar
350 g/12 oz plain flour
20 ml/4 teaspoons baking powder
2.5 ml/1/2 teaspoon ground
    cinnamon
30 ml/2 tablespoons vegetable oil
2 eggs
250 ml/8 fl oz milk
500 ml/18 fl oz water
vegetable oil, for frying
salt

Approximately per portion:
3,200 kJ/760 kcal
24 g protein, 34 g fat
84 g carbohydrate

● Approximate preparation
   time: 40 minutes

---

1. Coarsely pound the peanuts in a mortar with a pestle. Dry-fry the peanuts, together with the sesame seeds, in a heavy-based frying pan over a high heat, stirring constantly, for about 2 minutes. Remove the pan from the heat and stir in 60 ml/4 tablespoons of the sugar.

2. Put the remaining sugar in a bowl, together with the flour and baking powder. Add the cinnamon, a pinch of salt, the vegetable oil and eggs and mix well. Gradually stir in the milk and water to make a smooth, thin batter.

3. Heat a little vegetable oil in a large frying pan. Add a ladle of the batter and tilt the pan so that it covers the base. Fry the pancake over a medium heat for about 1 minute. Then sprinkle 30 ml/ 2 tablespoons of the peanut and sesame seed mixture over it. Cover and cook the pancake for a further 1–2 minutes. Fold it in half and slide it out of the frying pan. Keep warm until all the pancakes are cooked.

Above: Green pancakes with coconut filling
Below: Nut and sesame seed pancakes

Manioc cake

Bingkang ubi kaju

You can buy manioc in Asian and Caribbean food stores. It is also known as cassava.

For guests

Makes one 25–30 cm/10–12 inch cake
1.5 kg/3–3¹/₂ lb manioc
2 eggs
300 g/11 oz sugar
400 ml/14 fl oz coconut milk
butter, for greasing
salt

For 8 pieces approximately per piece:
3,100 kJ/740 kcal
3 g protein, 2 g fat
180 g carbohydrate

● Approximate preparation time: 2¹/₂ hours of which 1¹/₂ hours are cooling time

---

1. Peel and finely grate the manioc and squeeze out any liquid. Grease a shallow 25–30 cm/10–12 inch square cake or Swiss roll tin.

2. Beat the eggs with a pinch of salt with a hand-held electric mixer until foamy. Gradually add the sugar, beating constantly. Gradually add the coconut milk and the grated manioc, beating constantly.

3. Put the mixture in a non-stick pan and bring to the boil over a medium heat. Cook, stirring constantly, for about 5 minutes, until it becomes thick and smooth.

4. Put the manioc mixture into the prepared tin, smooth the surface and bake in a preheated oven at 220°C/425°F/Gas 7 for about 45 minutes, or until the top is golden brown.

5. Remove the cake from the oven, set aside to cool and cut it into 8 slices.

Black rice pudding

Nasi hitam

Sticky rice may be black – unpolished – or white and is popular in desserts. It is available from Chinese foodstores and many supermarkets.

Easy

Serves 4
250 g/9 oz black glutinous rice
750 ml/1¹/₄ pints coconut milk
115 g/4 oz palm sugar
200 ml/7 fl oz water

Approximately per portion:
1,300 kJ/310 kcal
5 g protein, 1 g fat
77 g carbohydrate

● Approximate preparation time: 2 hours 40 minutes of which 2 hours are soaking time

---

1. Rinse the rice in a strainer, drain and transfer to a bowl. Pour in enough water to cover the rice by 1 cm/¹/₂ inch. Set aside to soak for about 2 hours.

2. Drain the rice thoroughly and transfer to a saucepan with a tight-fitting lid. Add thecocnut milk, palm sugar and water. Bring to the boil over a high heat. Reduce the heat, cover and simmer over a low heat for about 30 minutes, until all the liquid has been absorbed. Serve the rice warm or cold.

Tip

It looks decorative if you garnish the black rice with a few slices of mango and rambutan fruits.

Above: Black rice pudding
Below: Manioc cake

Mangoes with a fragrant mould

Mangga buah buah

Easy

Serves 4
2 mangoes
15 g/¹/₂ oz agar-agar in one piece,
  about 15 cm/6 inches
800 ml/1 pint 8 fl oz water
300 ml/¹/₂ pint milk
150 g/5 oz sugar
30 ml/2 tablespoons almond or
  vanilla essence
mint leaves, to decorate

Approximately per portion:
1,300 kJ/310 kcal
3 g protein, 3 g fat
64 g carbohydrate

- Soaking time: at least
  12 hours
- Approximate preparation
  time: 40 minutes
- Cooling time: at least
  4 hours

---

1. On the day before, chill the mangoes in the refrigerator. Cut the agar-agar into 2 cm/³/₄ inch long pieces and soak them for about 12 hours or overnight in 500 ml/18 fl oz of the water.

2. The next day put the milk in a saucepan, together with the sugar and remaining water, and bring to the boil. Squeeze out the agar-agar pieces and add them to the saucepan. Bring to the boil again and then simmer over a low heat, stirring constantly, for about 5 minutes.

3. Remove the pan from the heat and set aside to cool for about 20 minutes.

4. Stir in the almond or vanilla essence. Rinse out a mould or basin with cold water and pour the mixture into it.

5. Cover the mould and chill in the refrigerator for at least 4 hours, until set. Peel the mangoes and cut the flesh into thin slices along the stones. Discard the stones.

6. Briefly dip the base of the mould in hot water and turn it out on to a serving plate. Arrange the mango slices beside it.

Coconut milk mould

Buah buah santen

For guests

Serves 4
20 g/³/₄ oz agar-agar in one piece,
  about 20 cm/8 inches
500 ml/18 fl oz water
750 ml/1¹/₄ pints coconut milk
250 g/9 oz sugar
5 drops red food colouring

Approximately per portion:
1,100 kJ/260 kcal
1 g protein, 0 g fat
66 g carbohydrate

- Soaking time: at least
  12 hours
- Approximate preparation
  time: 35 minutes
- Cooling time: at least
  4 hours

---

1. On the day before, cut the agar-agar into 2 cm/³/₄ inch long pieces and soak them for about 12 hours or overnight in the water.

2. Next day, bring the coconut milk to the boil in a saucepan, together with the sugar and the food colouring. Squeeze out the agar-agar pieces and add them to the pan. Bring to the boil again and simmer over a low heat, stirring constantly, for about 5 minutes.

3. Remove the pan from the heat and set aside to cool for about 20 minutes.

4. Rinse out a rectangular dish with cold water. Pour the mixture into it and chill in the refrigerator for at least 4 hours, until set.

5. Briefly dip the base of the dish in hot water. Turn out the coconut milk mould, cut it into 4 cm/1¹/₂ inch cubes and arrange on a serving plate.

Tip

It tastes delicious and looks attractive if you sprinkle the mould with toasted flakes of coconut.

Above: Mangoes with a fragrant mould
Below: Coconut milk mould

Steamed custard

Serikaja

Exquisite

Serves 4
butter, for greasing
3 eggs
115 g/4 oz palm sugar
400 ml/14 fl oz coconut milk
2.5 ml/1/2 teaspoon vanilla sugar
salt
30 ml/2 tablespoons grated coconut,
to decorate

Approximately per portion:
860 kJ/200 kcal
6 g protein, 6 g fat
32 g carbohydrate

● Approximate preparation
  time: 40 minutes

---

1. Grease 4 ramekins or small cups with butter. Put the eggs and the palm sugar into a bowl and beat them with a hand-held electric mixer until foamy. Mix in the coconut milk, vanilla sugar and a pinch of salt. Divide the mixture between the ramekins or cups.

2. Place the ramekins or cups side by side in a steamer set over a saucepan of boiling water. Cover and steam the custards over a low heat for about 30 minutes.

3. Remove the ramekins or cups from the steamer and set aside to cool completely. Just before serving, sprinkle them with the grated coconut.

Tip

You can also cook the custards in half coconut shells.

Sweet balls

Onde onde

Exquisite • Rather
time-consuming

Makes 45 balls
3 drops of daun pandan essence or
* green food colouring*
250 ml/8 fl oz water
250 g/9 oz sticky rice flour
75 g/3 oz hard palm sugar
115 g/4 oz grated coconut
salt

For 45 balls approximately
per ball:
150 kJ/36 kcal
0 g protein, 0 g fat
8 g carbohydrate

● Approximate preparation
  time: 1 1/4 hours

---

1. Mix the daun pandan essence or green food colouring with the water. Add the sticky rice flour and a pinch of salt. Mix thoroughly to form a dough. Knead the dough well until it becomes smooth and elastic.

2. Bring a saucepan of well-salted water to the boil. Dice the palm sugar into 5 mm/1/4 inch cubes.

---

3. Divide the dough into three portions. Form 15 balls from 1 portion and set the remaining dough aside. Press a hollow in the middle of each ball with your fingertip. Insert 1 cube of palm sugar and then press the dough together again.

4. Put the balls into a pan of boiling water. Reduce the heat and cook them over a low heat, turning occasionally, for about 15 minutes.

5. The balls are cooked when they rise to the surface. Carefully take them out of the water with a slotted spoon. Drain them, roll them in grated coconut and put on a plate.

6. Form another 15 balls from the second portion of dough, stuff them and cook them in the same way. Then do the same with the last portion of dough.

Tip

Never prepare all the balls for cooking at once because the dough becomes crumbly and the sugar melts.

Above: Sweet balls
Below: Steamed custard

Great Little Cook Books
Indonesian Cooking

Published originally under the title
Indonesisch kochen by Gräfe und
Unzer Verlag GmbH, München

© 1994 by Gräfe und Unzer Verlag
GmbH, München

English-language edition
© 1999 by Transedition Limited,
Oxford, England

This edition published by
Aura Books plc

Translation:
Translate-A-Book, Oxford

Editing:
Linda Doeser

Typesetting:
Organ Graphic, Abingdon

10 9 8 7 6 5 4 3 2 1
Printed in Dubai

ISBN 1 901683 12 5

Front cover illustration: You will
find the recipe for Fried rice on
page 20.

Note:
For all recipes, ingredients are
given in metric and imperial
measurements. Follow only one
set, as they are not
interchangeable.

Kusuma Widjaya
was born in Jakarta and spent his
childhood on Java. While he was
studying in Europe, he conceived
the idea of writing an Indonesian
cookery book. Today Kusuma
Widjaya runs a hotel restaurant on
Bali, offering local specialities. For
this book he has chosen classic
Indonesian dishes and many of his
favourite recipes.

Roland Marske
lives in Berlin. He studied
geography and political science
and travelled widely, mainly in
Asia and Africa, before becoming
a freelance journalist and
photographer. He co-operated
with his friend Kusuma Widjaya
to produce this book, to which
he contributed many photographs
as well as his profound knowledge
about the country and the people
of Indonesia.

Odette Teubner
was taught by her father, the
internationally renowned food
photographer, Christian Teubner.
After that, she worked for some
months as a fashion photographer.
At present, she works exclusively
in the Teubner Studio for Food
Photography. In her spare time she
is an enthusiastic painter of
children's portraits. She uses her
own son as a model.

Dorothee Gödert
When she had finished her studies
in photography, she started work
as a photographer of still life and
interiors. After spending some
time in Princeton in the United
States, she specialized in food
photography. She has worked with
several well-known food
photographers and now works in
the Teubner Studio for Food
Photography.